LIVING WITH THE DINOSAURS

SHARKS

LIVED WITH THE DINOSAURS!

BY JILL KEPPELER

Gareth Stevens
PUBLISHING

Please visit our website, www.garethstevens.com. For a free color catalog of all our high-quality books, call toll free 1-800-542-2595 or fax 1-877-542-2596.

Cataloging-in-Publication Data

Names: Keppeler, Jill.
Title: Sharks lived with the dinosaurs! / Jill Keppeler.
Description: New York : Gareth Stevens Publishing, 2017. | Series: Living with the dinosaurs | Includes index.
Identifiers: ISBN 9781482456752 (pbk.) | ISBN 9781482456790 (library bound) | ISBN 9781482456769 (6 pack)
Subjects: LCSH: Sharks–Juvenile literature. | Sharks, Fossil–Juvenile literature.
Classification: LCC QL638.9 K47 2017 | DDC 597.3–dc23

Published in 2017 by
Gareth Stevens Publishing
111 East 14th Street, Suite 349
New York, NY 10003

Designer: Laura Bowen
Editor: Therese Shea

Photo credits: Cover, p. 1 (shark) Wayne Lynch/All Canada Photos/Getty Images; cover, p. 1 (footprints) nemlaza/Shutterstock.com; cover, pp. 1–24 (background) Natalia Davidovich/Shutterstock.com; cover, pp. 1–24 (stone boxes) Daria Yakovleva/Shutterstock.com; p. 4 Alena Hovorkova/Shutterstock.com; p. 5 solarseven/Shutterstock.com; p. 7 (top) De Agostini Picture Library/Getty Images; p. 7 (bottom) Linda Bucklin/Shutterstock.com; p. 8 Sytillin Pavel/Shutterstock.com; p. 9 Havoc/Shutterstock.com; p. 10 NobuTamura/Wikimedia Commons; pp. 11 (*Hybodus*), 12, 21 (*Megalodon*) Herschel Hoffmeyer/Shutterstock.com; p. 11 (Ginsu tooth) A,Ocram/Wikimedia Commons; p. 11 (Ginsu shark) Lomita/Wikimedia Commons; p. 13 Michael Rosskothen/Shutterstock.com; p. 15 (top) Slick-o-bot/Wikimedia Commons; p. 15 (bottom) DiBgd/Wikimedia Commons; p. 17 (top) Tomas Kotouc/Shutterstock.com; p. 17 (bottom left) Bob Orsillo/Shutterstock.com; p. 17 (bottom right) Catmando/Shutterstock.com; p. 19 Matt9122/Shutterstock.com; p. 20 Jim Agronick/Shutterstock.com.

Printed in the United States of America

CPSIA compliance information: Batch #CW17GS: For further information contact Gareth Stevens, New York, New York at 1-800-542-2595.

CONTENTS

Words in the glossary appear in **bold** type the first time they are used in the text.

A LONG, LONG TIME AGO

When you think of creatures from a very long time ago, you probably think of dinosaurs. These ancient **reptiles** first walked our planet about 245 million years ago. Dinosaurs stomped, flew, and even swam for many years on Earth. By about 65 million years ago, however, they had died out or **evolved** into other animals.

Another amazing animal swam in Earth's oceans millions of years before dinosaurs existed—and forms of that killer creature still live today. Let's learn about **prehistoric** sharks!

THERE ARE BIGGER CREATURES IN THE OCEANS, BUT SHARKS HAVE MANY **ADAPTATIONS** THAT MAKE THEM THE KINGS OF THE SEA. MORE THAN 400 SPECIES, OR KINDS, OF SHARKS ARE ALIVE TODAY.

THE FIRST SHARKS?

No one is sure when sharks first appeared. There's **evidence** the first sharklike fish lived more than 400 million years ago. Sharks then were different from the sharks of today. The early shark *Cladoselache* (klad-uh-SEHL-uh-kee) had a mouth at the front of its head rather than on the bottom of its head, as sharks today have.

Modern sharks first appeared during the Jurassic period, which began about 200 million years ago. By the Cretaceous period, which began about 145 million years ago, sharks looked much like they do today.

THE PREHISTORIC WORLD

Some dinosaurs were smaller than the sharks that lived during the same time. *Compsognathus* (kahmp-SAHG-nuh-thus) was one of the smallest dinosaurs. It grew about as tall as a chicken, but was about 2 to 3 feet (0.6 to 0.9 m) long.

MOST ANCIENT AND ALL MODERN SHARKS HAVE TOOTHLIKE SCALES FOR PROTECTION. HOWEVER, *CLADOSELACHE* DIDN'T HAVE THESE SCALES. IT HAD A SHORT, ROUNDED **SNOUT**, TOO.

THE TOOTH IS OUT THERE

Scientists have discovered about 1,000 species of dinosaurs so far—but they've found 2,000 to 3,000 species of prehistoric sharks! They've learned a lot about these sharks because of something the sharks left behind—their teeth.

A shark's skeleton is made of **cartilage**, which breaks down after the shark dies. However, shark teeth often turn into **fossils**. Fossilized teeth can tell a scientist how big a shark was, where it lived, what it ate, and how long ago it lived.

THE PREHISTORIC WORLD

The earliest known shark teeth are from 400 million years ago. They had two points and were very small.

SHARKS LOSE AND REPLACE THOUSANDS OF TEETH OVER THEIR LIFETIME. THAT'S ALSO A USEFUL ADAPTATION FOR MEAT EATERS!

BAD BITERS

One shark that shared Earth with the dinosaurs was *Hybodus* (HYB-uh-duhs). This shark, which lived about 180 million years ago, had two kinds of teeth—sharp ones for biting sea creatures and flat ones for breaking shells. *Hybodus* also had a bony blade on its back fin to warn off predators.

Cretoxyrhina (kreh-tox-ee-RY-nuh) appeared about 100 million years ago. Also called the Ginsu shark, the creature got this nickname because of its teeth. The word "Ginsu" is the name of a supersharp knife.

Xenacanthus

THE PREHISTORIC WORLD

Sharks from the group *Xenacanthus* (zee-nah-KAN-thus) looked like eels with a spine sticking out of their head!

Hybodus

Ginsu shark tooth

CRETOXYRHINA, OR THE GINSU SHARK, COULD GROW UP TO 24 FEET (7.3 M) LONG.

Ginsu shark

PREDATORS AND PREY

Sometimes, dinosaurs ate ancient sharks. *Spinosaurus* (spyn-oh-SAWR-uhs), a huge dinosaur that lived about 95 million years ago, could swim and probably enjoyed dining on sharks. Mosasaurs (MOH-suh-sawrz), reptiles that swam in ancient oceans, also probably ate sharks.

Sometimes, sharks ate dinosaurs! Scientists have found ancient shark teeth in fossilized dinosaur bones. So far, there's no evidence that sharks killed the dinosaurs they ate. However, that doesn't mean it never happened. Sharks swam through rivers and lakes that dinosaurs might have drunk from.

Spinosaurus

MOSASAURS WEREN'T DINOSAURS, BUT THEY WERE BIG. THEY COULD GROW UP TO 50 FEET (15 M) LONG!

THE PREHISTORIC WORLD

Spinosaurus was one of the largest meat-eating dinosaurs to ever live on Earth. This creature lived in North Africa. It had long spines growing out of its back to form a body part that looked like a sail.

THE SCAVENGER

Squalicorax (skwal-ih-KOHR-ax) lived during the same time as *Cretoxyrhina*, about 100 million years ago. Some scientists think *Squalicorax* was probably a scavenger, or an animal that eats **carrion**. That's why *Squalicorax* is sometimes called a crow shark.

Scientists believe *Squalicorax* was a scavenger because they've found this shark's tooth in mosasaur remains. The reptile was likely dead before the shark found it. Scavenging would have helped *Squalicorax* survive during times when it was hard to find live prey.

THE PREHISTORIC WORLD

In 2015, a team of scientists announced the discovery of *Pseudomegachasma* (soo-doh-mehg-uh-KAS-muh), which lived about 100 million years ago. This shark had a huge mouth and ate tiny sea creatures. It had lots of very small teeth.

REMAINS OF A *SQUALICORAX* WERE FOUND IN KANSAS! WE KNOW MUCH OF THIS LAND WAS ONCE UNDERWATER.

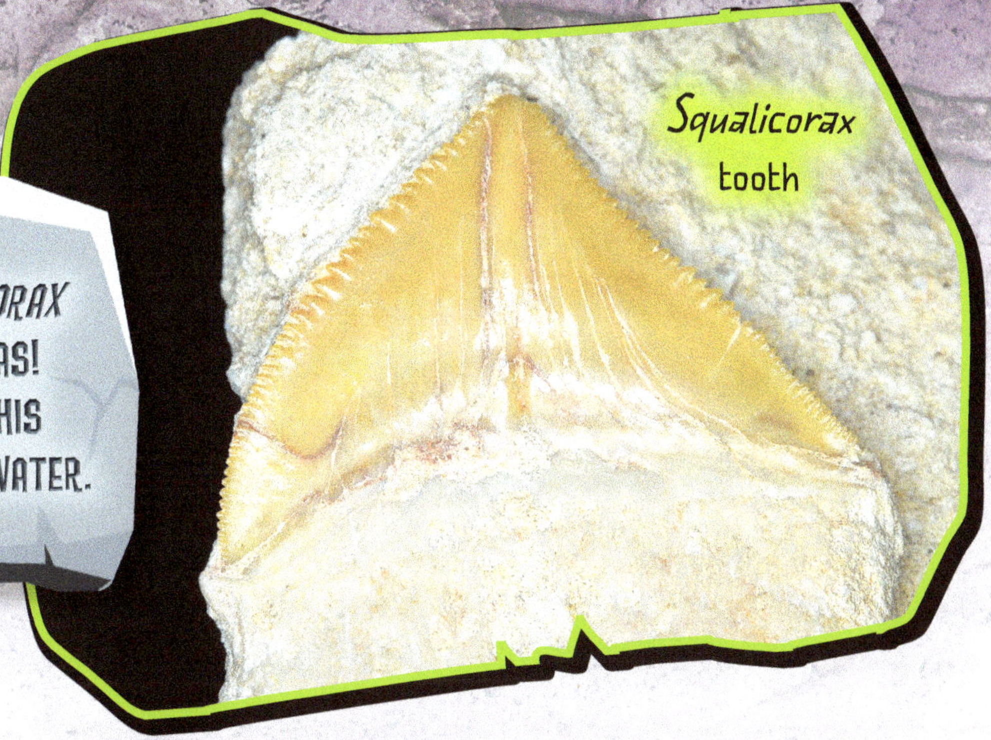

Squalicorax tooth

Squalicorax

ESCAPING EXTINCTION

Throughout the history of Earth, there have been five mass **extinction** events, which are fast and widespread losses of life across the planet. The mass extinction event that occurred about 65 million years ago led to the extinction of the large dinosaurs, and about 80 percent of animal species!

Sharks have survived all five of these terrible events. What makes sharks such great survivors? Adaptations are the key. Sharks passed on features and **behaviors** that helped them live in their watery worlds.

THE PREHISTORIC WORLD

Although they weren't dinosaurs, ichthyosaurs (IHK-thee-uh-sawrz) and plesiosaurs (PLEE-see-uh-sawrz) were large reptiles during the time of the dinosaurs. They shared waters with sharks. Ichthyosaurs looked much like today's porpoises. Plesiosaurs had long necks and fins.

HAMMERHEAD SHARKS ARE VERY STRANGE-LOOKING SHARKS. THE HAMMERHEAD SHARK'S ODD HEAD SHAPE IS PROBABLY AN ADAPTATION THAT HELPS IT SMELL AND SEE BETTER IN ITS OCEAN WORLD.

SHARK SURVIVORS

Sharks survived an extinction event that took place about 250 million years ago. It was so terrible it was called the "Great Dying." We don't know what happened to cause this extinction event, but scientists think 96 percent of all species in the world died!

Sharks may have escaped this extinction event by swimming deeper in the ocean. There, they could hide from deadly surface conditions. Sharks lived in these depths for a long time, adapting to eat creatures that lived in these deeper waters.

THE PREHISTORIC WORLD

Shark jaws changed so they could more easily catch prey—and bigger prey. Today's sharks can **detach** their upper jaw from their skull and push it out to grab prey.

WHEN MODERN SHARK JAWS OPEN, THEY CREATE A SPACE THAT SUCKS IN PREY—LIKE A VACUUM!

SHARKS TODAY

After the dinosaurs died out, the largest sharks ruled the seas. *Megalodon* (MEHG-uh-luh-dahn) grew to more than 45 feet (14 m) long and may have weighed up to 50 tons (45 mt). It probably ate whales! However, this shark became extinct about 2 million years ago.

While many sharks evolved or became extinct, a few kinds that lived during the time of the dinosaurs are still around today. Modern frilled sharks are just like frilled sharks of 80 million years ago. Sharks like these are true survivors!

great white shark

GREAT WHITE SHARKS OF TODAY ARE MUCH LIKE *MEGALODON*, BUT THEY DON'T GROW QUITE AS LARGE.

A SHARK TIMELINE

Megalodon

450 — The earliest sharklike fish date back to this time.

420 — Scientists agree the earliest true sharks come from this time.

250 — Sharks survive "The Great Dying" mass extinction event.

245 — The first dinosaurs appeared on Earth.

200 — Sharks with modern features swim Earth's waters.

80 — Frilled sharks date back to this time.

65 — A mass extinction event wipes out the dinosaurs.

MILLION YEARS AGO

GLOSSARY

adaptation: a change in an animal that makes it better able to live in its surroundings

behavior: the way an animal acts

carrion: a dead, rotting animal

cartilage: tough, bendable tissue that makes up part or all of a skeleton

detach: to separate

evidence: something that shows that something else is true

evolve: to grow and change over time

extinction: the death of all members of a species

fossil: the hardened marks or remains of plants and animals that formed over thousands or millions of years

prehistoric: having to do with the time before written history

reptile: an animal covered with scales or plates that breathes air, has a backbone, and lays eggs, such as a turtle, snake, lizard, or crocodile

snout: an animal's nose and mouth

FOR MORE INFORMATION

BOOKS

Bonner, Hannah. *When Fish Got Feet, When Bugs Were Big, & When Dinos Dawned: A Cartoon Prehistory of Life on Earth.* Washington, DC: National Geographic Society, 2015.

Discovery Channel. *Sharkopedia: The Complete Guide to Everything Shark.* Des Moines, IA: Time Home Entertainment, 2013.

Musgrave, Ruth. *National Geographic Kids Everything Sharks.* Washington, DC: National Geographic, 2011.

WEBSITES

The Evolution of Sharks
www.enchantedlearning.com/subjects/sharks/allabout/evolution.shtml
This website has facts about ancient and modern-day sharks.

How Sharks Survived the "Great Dying"
www.sciencenewsforstudents.org/article/how-sharks-survived-great-dying
Learn about sharks and the biggest extinction event in Earth's history.

The Strange and Terrifying World of Prehistoric Sharks
sharkopedia.discovery.com/shark-topics/prehistoric-sharks/
This website offers a look at more than 400 million years of shark history.

INDEX